UNITED STATES

DEPARTMENT OF THE INTERIOR

OFFICE OF AIRCRAFT SERVICES

300 E. Mallard Dr., Suite 200
Boise, Idaho 83706-3991

AVIATION FUEL HANDLING

HANDBOOK

AVIATION FUEL HANDLING HANDBOOK
(351 DM 1)

FOREWORD

This Departmental Manual Handbook, as authorized in 351 DM 1, sets forth the objectives, standards, specifications and procedures of the Interior Aviation Fuel Quality Control Program.

Questions regarding the content of this Handbook may be directed to the Aviation Safety Manager, Office of the Director, Office of Aircraft Services (OAS), P.O. Box 15428, Boise, Idaho 83715-5428 or the Alaska Regional Director, Office of Aircraft Services, 4837 Aircraft Drive, Anchorage, Alaska 99502-1052. Additional copies of the Handbook may be obtained from OAS at the same addresses.

/s/ Ben Campbell
Director, OAS

Date: *1/3/94*

AVIATION FUEL HANDLING HANDBOOK
(351 DM 1)

TABLE OF CONTENTS

Page

Chapter 1   General Information 1
.1 Objectives 1
.2 Authority 1
.3 Policy 1
.4 Responsibility 1
.5 Fuel or Oil Pollution Prevention 2
.6 Deviations/Waivers 2

Chapter 2   Identification of Aviation Fuels 3
.1 Color-Coding 3
.2 Marking 3
.3 Summary 4

Chapter 3   Quality Control 5
.1 Quality Control 5
.2 Responsibility 6
.3 Department of Defense (DOD) Fuel Services 6
.4 Commercial Fuel Services 6
.5 Fuel Sampling and Testing 7
.6 Sampling After Aircraft Accidents/Selected Serious Incidents 7

Chapter 4   Filtration 9
.1 Policy 9
.2 General 9
.3 Filter Considerations 9
.4 Filter Types 10
.5 Filter Applications 11
.6 Differential Pressure 11
.7 Filter Change-Out Criteria 12

Chapter 5   Standards 13
.1 Quality of Product 13
.2 Technical Requirements - Fuel Servicing Equipment 13
.3 Fixed Facility Basic Design Criteria 14

Chapter 6   Bonding 16
.1 General 16
.2 Static Electricity 16
.3 Bonding 16
.4 Plastic 16
.5 Bonding Procedures 16
.6 Special Considerations When Handling Turbine Fuels 17
.7 Other Special Considerations/Procedures 17
.8 Equipment for Bonding 17

AVIATION FUEL HANDLING HANDBOOK
(351 DM 1)

TABLE OF CONTENTS (continued)

	Page
Chapter 7 Government Fueling Operations	18
.1 General	18
.2 Responsibility	18
.3 Personnel Training	18
.4 Refueler Pre-Operational Checks	18
.5 Sequence of Operations	18
.6 Fuel Dispensing Operations	20
.7 Follow-up Emergency Fire and Rescue Procedures	23
.8 Fire Extinguisher Requirements	24
Chapter 8 Inspections	25
.1 General	25
.2 Daily Inspections or Prior to Use (All Filter Systems)	25
.3 Weekly Inspections	26
.4 Monthly Inspections	26
.5 Annual Inspections	27
.6 On-Site Inspection	27
.7 Alaska Region Operational Requirements	27
.8 Bureaus Purchase of Bulk Fuel	27
.9 Remote On-Site Fuel Tests	27
.10 Assistance	28
.11 Fuel Sampling Kit	28
.12 Fuel Lock Out-Tag Out (Government-owned, Operated, and Con-trolled)	28
Chapter 9 Fuel Contamination Reporting Procedures	29
.1 General	29
.2 Notification	29
.3 Investigation	29
.4 Follow-up Actions	29
Chapter 10 U S Department of Defense (DOD) Fuel Service Contracting	30
.1 General	30
.2 Policy	30
.3 Defense Fuel Supply Centers	30
.4 Inspection of DFSC Delivered Fuels	30
Chapter 11 Inventories and Reporting of Government-owned Aviation Fuels	31
.1 Form OAS-59	31
.2 Delivery	31
.3 Physical Inventories, Recordkeeping and Mailing to OAS	31
.4 Inventory Technique	32

Appendix A: Bibliography
Appendix B: Sources of Ignition
Appendix C: Fuel Sampling and Testing - Quality Control

NOTE: Certain portions of this Handbook were extracted from National Fire Protection Association (NFPA) 407 with permission as stipulated in the following acknowledgement: "Reproduced with permission from NFPA 407, Standard for Aircraft Fuel Servicing, 1990 edition, copyright 1990, National Fire Protection Association, 407 Atlantic
Avenue, Boston, MA 02210.

Chapter 1 General Information   1.1

1.1 <u>Objectives</u>. The objective of this Handbook is to establish the procedures, guidelines, and standards for the Department of the Interior (DOI) Aviation Fuel Quality Control Program. This should help assure the delivery of the correct type and grade of uncontaminated fuel into aircraft utilized for DOI aviation operations. The Office of Aircraft Services (OAS) will provide Department bureaus with:

   A.   Procurement services and direct ordering information and advice.

   B.   Technical advice on fuel systems, quality control and fuel transportation.

   C.   Technical training in handling, storage and dispensing of aviation fuels.

   D.   Periodic fuel quality control inspections.

   E.   Timely results of bureau fuel site(s) inspections.

   F.   Information on new innovations and the use of the latest equipment.

1.2 <u>Authority</u>. The authority for the establishment of this Handbook is specified in Departmental Manual 351 DM 1, <u>Flight Operations Standards and Procedures</u>.

1.3 <u>Policy</u>. To enhance the safety of DOI employees and of the public in general, all Departmental personnel responsible for the transportation, storage or dispensing of aviation fuels shall adhere to the guidelines, procedures and standards prescribed within this Handbook.

1.4 <u>Responsibility</u>.

   A.   <u>Management</u>. Bureau Directors are ultimately responsible for the management and effective implementation of the Interior Aviation Fuel Quality Control Program within their bureau. Supervisors and managers at all levels are responsible for the safe delivery of uncontaminated aviation fuels during aviation operations under their jurisdiction or control. Within this responsibility is the practical requirement to provide safe working conditions, prevention of injury to persons, and the protection of property.

   B.   <u>DOI Employees</u>. To enhance safety, Departmental employees who become aware of any fuel-related mishaps such as excessive spills, fires, damage to aircraft or fueling vehicles/facilities, etc., during fueling operations, shall report such occurrences utilizing Form OAS-34, <u>Aviation Mishap Information System</u>. Imminent danger situations shall be handled and reported as specified in 29 CFR 1960 and 485 DM 1, as supplemented by bureau policy.

   C.   <u>Fuel Contractors</u>. Companies conducting business for the transportation, storage or dispensing of aviation fuels, including into-aircraft operations, shall adhere to the provisions and specifications for such operations as provided within the contract or agreement. For the most part, all such operations shall be in accordance with the standards/procedures specified in appropriate ANSI (American National Standard Institute) or NFPA (National Fire Protection Association) publications.

D. Pilots. All pilots flying for the U.S. Department of the Interior is ultimately responsible for ensuring that the proper type and grade of clean, dry fuel is pumped into their aircraft.

1.5 Fuel or Oil Pollution Prevention. Bureaus must be cognizant of the Environmental Protection Agency's (EPA) regulations found in 40 CFR 112. Regardless of the size or location of an operation, it is necessary that an assessment be made to determine whether or not provisions of the oil pollution regulations are applicable. Basically, the criteria is if it can be reasonably expected that a discharge of fuel or oil will enter navigable waters, a facility is subject to the regulations. These regulations require the preparation and implementation of a Spill Prevention Control and Countermeasure (SPCC) Plan. The exceptions to this requirement are:

A. Aboveground. Facilities having a total aboveground storage capacity of 1,320 gallons or less of fuel, provided no single container has a capacity in excess of 660 gallons (see Appendix A.16).

B. Underground. Facilities having a total storage capacity of less than 42,000 gallons.

NOTE: Bureaus are urged to contact their local EPA office for detailed information concerning these regulations. (See Appendices A.16 and A.17.)

1.6 Deviations/Waivers. Should a deviation from any part of this Handbook, be necessary, a request for waiver shall be addressed to the Director, Office of Aircraft Services, P.O. Box 15428, Boise, Idaho 83715-5428. If a contract specification/provision is involved, the appropriate individual to contact is the Contracting Officer in either the Boise or Anchorage offices. This request must contain justification, possible alternate procedures and must not compromise safety of personnel or environment.

2.1 <u>Color-Coding</u>. There are two categories of aviation fuel in use today: aviation gasoline (commonly called AVGAS) and turbine or jet-fuel.

A.   <u>Aviation Gasoline (AVGAS)</u>. Aviation gasolines are used in reciprocating engine aircraft. There are currently two grades of aviation gasoline in use: 100 low lead and 100/130. Off-colored fuel may not meet specifications and should not be used for aviation purposes unless samples have been taken and are laboratory approved.   The following various grades of aviation gasoline are dyed different colors to aid recognition.

   (1) Blue - 100 low lead (100LL)

   (2) Green - 100/130

B.   <u>Turbine Fuel/Jet Fuel</u>. Aviation turbine fuels are used for powering turbo-fan, turbojet and turboprop engines. There are two types of turbine fuel in use: A kerosene base (Jet A, Jet A-50, JP-8, and Jet A-1), and a blend of gasoline and kerosene (Jet B and JP-4). Most commercial operators utilize Jet A or Jet A-50, and the military normally uses JP-4 and JP-8. The specifications for JP-8 are similar to Jet A except that JP-8 has required additives for anti-icing, corrosion inhibitor, and anti-static. All grades of turbine fuels are colorless or straw-colored.

2.2 <u>Marking</u>. In addition to coloring the fuels, a marking and coding system has been adopted to identify the various airport fuel handling facilities, pieces of equipment, containers, inlets-outlets-joints, and aircraft fuel filler openings according to the type and grade of fuel they contain. Reference API Bulletin 1542 (see Appendix A.19).

A.   <u>Fuelers</u>. Each aircraft fuel servicing vehicle shall be conspicuously and legibly marked with an identification decal to indicate the product contained therein. The markings shall be on each side and the rear of the fueler tank in letters at least 3" in height.

   (1) Aviation gasolines are identified by using white letters on a blue background for 100LL or white letters on a green background for 100/130.

   (2) Turbine fuels are identified by using white letters on a black background, i.e., Jet A or Jet B.

   (3) Vehicles must be marked on both sides and on the rear of the tank.
        JET A - Combustible   JET B - Flammable   AVGAS - Flammable

B.   <u>Valves and Piping at Permanent Storage Facilities</u>. Valves, loading and unloading connections, switches and other control equipment shall be color-coded to identify the grade and type of fuel they control. The fuel in piping is identified by name and by painted colored bands or a decal placed around the pipe at intervals along its length.

C. Hose Lines. Hose lines shall be marked by decals or labeled adjacent to the nozzle to indicate the type of fuel dispensed. Reference American Petroleum Institute Bulletin 1542 (see Appendix A.19).

D. Portable Storage Facilities - Containers.

(1) Bulk Collapsible Tanks (bladders and rollagons). Large fixed collapsible tanking facilities, their accessory fueling lines and equipment shall be marked or decal attached in accordance with paragraphs 2.2A(1), (2), and (3).

(2) 250- and 500-Gallon Collapsible Rollagons. Each end of a rollagon shall be marked in letters at least 4" high with the type and/or grade of fuel in the container.

(3) 55-Gallon Barrels. The top head or sides of 55-gallon barrels shall be marked in letters no smaller than 3/4" with the type and/or grade of fuel, filling date, vendor and any other pertinent information required.

(4) 5-Gallon and Smaller Containers. All containers shall be marked with the type and/or grade of fuel contained in the containers. In many cases the 5-gallon containers will be marked by the fuel manufacturer.

CAUTION: Plastic containers are not to be used for into-aircraft refueling as the static electricity charge potential is sufficient to cause a spark with potential explosive results. (See paragraphs 6.2, 6.4 and Appendix B).

E. Aircraft. Various Federal Aviation Regulations (FARs) require that aircraft fuel filler openings be marked to show the word "FUEL," the minimum fuel grade or designation for the engines, and the tank capacity. In order that these markings retain their effectiveness, regulations require that they be kept fresh and clean. Therefore, frequent washing and occasional painting will be necessary to retain clear legibility.

2.3 Summary. The maintenance of fuel quality requires vigilance at every stage of handling. All components of any type fueling facility and equipment shall be identified and keyed to the marking and color-code system.

Chapter 3 Quality Control   **3.1**

3.1 <u>Quality Control</u>. The quality and cleanliness of aviation fuels are vital to the safety of DOI aircraft and, subsequently, all flight personnel.

A. <u>General</u>. Fine sediment in fuel may block the engine fuel supply system and erode critical parts in the engine and fuel control systems. Free water (water not dissolved in the fuel) may freeze at high altitudes or cold outside air temperatures and plug the fuel screens, causing the engine to cease operation/flame out and possible loss of the aircraft. Salt water is extremely dangerous because of its potential effect on certain aircraft instruments. Contaminants must be separated out of fuel before the fuel is pumped into the aircraft.

B. <u>Requirements</u>. The following items are related to aviation fuel quality surveillance and directly effect aviation safety within Department of the Interior.

(1) All fuel quality assurance and equipment maintenance records for equipment and facilities of fuel storage and delivery operations shall be available for inspection during normal working hours.

(2) If visible contamination is found, fueling will be discontinued immediately and the bureau designated representative or the OAS Fuel Quality Control Specialist notified. Fueling shall not be resumed from the system until the source of contamination is found and removed. Pilots of other aircraft fueled from this source shall be notified immediately.

(3) If for any reason a fueling system becomes inoperative so as to impair aircraft operations, the nearest OAS Regional/Area Office should be contacted.

(4) All inspections and tests specified in this document, other than personal pilot into-aircraft refueling, should be performed by designated personnel properly trained to do so.

(5) The bureau making the fuel available to into-aircraft refueling vehicles, trailers or aircraft, is responsible for assuring that all fuel handling personnel are properly trained.

(6) Fuel which is removed from an aircraft because of possible contamination shall be held in quarantine until laboratory tests have been performed to determine its acceptability. Such fuel may be used for non-aviation purposes, provided it is properly identified and controlled.

(7) Immediately following any aircraft accident or incident where an engine problem was encountered, every effort shall be made to determine the aircraft's last fueling point.

(a) If the fuel was obtained from a DOI fuel source, it is the responsibility of the senior bureau official at the fuel point to ensure the "LOCK OUT-TAG OUT" procedures are performed. Immediate notification procedures shall be initiated to notify the pilots of other aircraft known to have obtained fuel from this source to check the quality of the fuel in their aircraft.

(b) Only the OAS Aircraft Accident Investigator-in-Charge (IIC) or the OAS Alaska Regional Director can authorize entry into the fuel "LOCK OUT." The senior bureau official on site shall be responsible for ensuring the "LOCK OUT" until representative sampling is completed, and proper testing performed on the fuel either released to further use or removed form service. **NOTE:** The senior official at the fuel point <u>SHALL IMMEDIATELY</u> determine which other aircraft were refueled from this source and notify the pilot to immediately check the quality of the fuel in their aircraft. For fuel supplied by other than DOI operations, notification of suspect fuel to the dispensing agent shall be made immediately.

(c) For fuel supplied by other than DOI sources, notification of suspect fuel to the dispensing vendor shall be made immediately. The DOI official shall attempt to learn of any other DOI aircraft that fueled from this source, and then request that a fuel sample be taken by the vendor and made available for testing by DOI.

3.2 <u>Responsibility.</u> Any bureau organization that has aviation fuel in its physical possession is responsible for establishing and maintaining an adequate fuel quality control or surveillance program. Each pilot involved in aircraft refueling is responsible for ensuring that the fuel pumped into an aircraft is of the proper type and grade, clean, bright, and free from contamination.

3.3 <u>Department of Defense (DOD) Fuel Services</u>. OAS purchases bulk fuel from the Defense Fuel Supply Centers (DFSC). Quality control policies and procedures rest with the Department of Defense until purchased by OAS and are addressed in chapter 10, <u>U.S. Department of Defense (DOD) Fuel Service Contract</u>.

3.4 <u>Commercial Fuel Services</u>. Commercial aviation fuels manufacturers provide guidelines and procedures to their dealerships/commercial fuel vendors, in some localities. With limited to non-existent oversight by the manufacturers, it is essential that the Interior aviation community police itself and be aware of potential fuel contamination problems. Additionally, neither the Department of Transportation (DOT) nor the Federal Aviation Administration (FAA) provide quality control surveillance over commercial vendors of aviation fuels products.

A. <u>Alertness During Refueling Operations</u>. Pilots must constantly be on the alert for non-approved aviation refueling equipment such as filters and nozzles. Refuelers may contain commingled fuels, and untrained personnel may be operating refuelers or fixed site facilities. There is always a potential for receiving incorrect type and grade or commingled fuel.

B. <u>OAS Inspection of Commercial Facilities</u>. Bureaus ordering directly from commercial vendors should establish an agreement with the vendor for an OAS representative to inspect the facility prior to bureau purchasing/utilizing fuels dispensed into their aircraft. This agreement is the only authority OAS will have to conduct on-site inspections of commercial operations.

C. <u>Discrepancies</u>. Under the process of the bureau directly ordering from the commercial vendor, the vendor is under no obligation to change equipment or procedures if determined to be unacceptable to DOI standards of operation. In the event such discrepancies are found, the OAS representative will:

(1) Provide the commercial vendor a written list of discrepancies along with recommendations for correction.

(2) Provide a copy of this list with recommendations to the bureau official requesting the OAS inspection. If such discrepancies are sufficient to so warrant, the OAS representative will provide a recommendation NOT TO USE the commercial vendor until critical discrepancies have been corrected.

(3) If the inspection is deemed "satisfactory," a letter will be provided to the bureau official requesting the inspection with a recommendation for USE of the fuel.

3.5 <u>Fuel Sampling and Testing</u>. Sampling and testing of aviation products must be accomplished during each phase of fuel transfer. This includes verification of fuel type and quality at the bulk dispensing facility pumping into DOI fuel transport vehicles or trailers, at the fuel storage facility being operated by the bureau, any fuel source in the refueler or trailer which shall be conducting into-aircraft refueling, and finally, fuel quality assurance prior to any into-aircraft fueling operations. DOI Fuel Quality Control Program sampling and testing information and procedures is provided for in detail in Appendix C, <u>Fuel Sampling and Testing Requirements - Fuel Quality Control</u>.

3.6 <u>Sampling After Aircraft Accidents/Selected Serious Incidents</u>. Fuel samples are taken after aircraft accidents and selected serious incidents. These samples are normally drawn by or under the direction of the OAS Investigator-In-Charge (IIC). Occasionally, the IIC may request assistance from OAS qualified maintenance personnel or fuel handling personnel to draw samples from the mishap aircraft and last known refueling facilities/sites. Bureau personnel may also be called upon to assist in the sampling of fuels. In most cases, coordination with the OAS IIC or the OAS Alaska Regional Office will be effected prior to any fuel sampling following an aircraft accident or serious incident. In some circumstances, it may be immediately necessary to take a fuel sample prior to this coordination effort. If this is the case, the following information should be adhered to during sampling. (See Appendix A.2).

A. <u>Sampling From Aircraft</u>. Fuel and lubricant samples should be taken from the aircraft as soon as possible after the mishap. Samples are to be taken as follows:

(1) A 1-gallon DOT-approved aviation fuel sampling can should be used. If these resources are not available, CLEAN - NEW containers can be used for drawing the fuel.

(2) One (1) gallon sample of fuel is to be drawn from the aircraft fuel sump. If the aircraft has tanks that do not flow into each other, samples must be taken from each tank's sump and containers marked to note the tank from which the fuel was drawn. Samples must be checked for color, visible water, sediment, and contaminants. All samples must be closed tightly and containers tagged **SUSPECT FUEL - AIRCRAFT ACCIDENT**, indicating the source(s) from which they were drawn (which tank), location, date, name of the individual drawing the sample (legible), with the aircraft registration number on the tag. All ambient conditions must be recorded at the time of the mishap.

Chapter 3 Quality Control   3.6A(3)

(3) These samples are to be forwarded as indicated by coordination with the OAS IIC or OAS Alaska Regional Office.

B. Sampling From Refueling Source. The fuel records history of the aircraft needs to be retraced. Procedures to obtain information and collect samples are as follows:

(1) The date of the last refueling before the mishap must be recorded, as well as the system or number of the refueler involved, location, and name of the organization or supplier of the service. If appropriate, the results of the filter efficiency and Aqua-Glo tests of the refueler as well as the daily filter pressure differential (psiD) readings, will need to be checked. A copy of the manufacturer's Fuel Analysis Report covering the Lot Number from which the suspect fuel was acquired must be obtained.

(2) The organization that provided the last refueling must be contacted, and information recorded to indicate the date that the applicable refueler, tank, trailer, rollagon, barrel, etc., was filled and the bulk storage system/facility from which it was filled.

(3) The organization responsible for the bulk storage system/facility must also be contacted. The date the fuel was received into the storage system and the supplier of the fuel need to be recorded. If the fuel in storage has not been tested for 90 days or more, it should be retested. Storage tank records should indicate daily water bottom checks and test results when products were received.

NOTE. The fuel source under control of DOI should be under a "LOCK OUT - TAG OUT" procedure at this time. Only the OAS IIC or OAS Alaska Regional Director can authorize entry for sampling or release of the fuel source for use. If so authorized, proceed with steps (4) and (5).

(4) One (1) gallon samples must be drawn from each of the following refueler locations: tank sump, filter sump, and hose nozzle; or if the aircraft was last refueled directly from other than a refueler (tank, rollagon, fixed fueling facility, barrel, etc.), a one (1) gallon sample must be drawn from the hose nozzle. Also, if possible, a one (1) gallon sample should be drawn from the supplying bulk storage outlet. All samples must be tightly closed and tagged as noted in A(2) above.

(5) Samples are to be forwarded as indicated by coordination with the OAS IIC or OAS Alaska Regional Office.

C. Sampling Kit. A general use fuel sampling kit should contain the following items:
(1) DOT-approved clean 1-gallon sample can.

(2) Sample tags, shipping tag, and labels.

(3) Four clear (glass), 4-ounce sample bottles to use for visual checks.

NOTE. Additional information regarding bureau responsibility is provided in chapter 8, Inspections.

Chapter 4 Filtration   4.1

4.1 <u>Policy</u>. All DOI owned, operated and maintained aircraft refueling facilities will have a filtration unit qualified to a current aviation industry standard or otherwise acceptable to a qualified OAS/DOI fuel quality control representative. All aircraft refueling will be done according to the filter manufacturers' operating specifications, the aircraft manufacturers' requirements, and this Handbook.

NOTE: Procurement personnel, pilots, mechanics, and contracting officers (see 4.5C, <u>CAUTION</u>).

4.2 <u>General</u>. DOI operates and contracts for a wide variety of make and model air-craft in every type of terrain, weather and cultural environment. Many of these aircraft engines and their fuel systems have been designed with some limited tolerance for particulates and water. For this reason the most important component in any aircraft refueling facility is the filtration system.

NOTE. Each pilot is required to consult the aircraft operators manual and engine capabilities and limitations section for each aircraft to be flown in order to determine if the resources present in the refueling system permit compliance with the aircraft requirements for the following:

(1) Type and grade of fuels approved.

(2) Type and amount of additives approved for use.

(3) Particulates in milligram per gallon (mg/G) or milligram per liter (mg/L) allowed, if stated.

(4) Water in parts per million (ppm) allowed, if stated.

(5) Any fuel related limitations to the fuel system components and engine.

4.3 <u>Filter Considerations</u>. There are three major filter considerations which shall be met. These are:

A. All filters must be "<u>aviation approved</u>" and identified in writing or placarding to meet the most current aviation petroleum industry standard. In North America, the two industry standards sought by filtration manufacturers are:

(1) <u>Institute of Petroleum (IP)</u>. For "Aviation Fuel Filter Monitors with Absorbent Type Elements," such as Velcon's <u>Aquacon Aviation Elements</u>.

NOTE. For all future references to single element monitors, it is understood they have met the requirements of the IP or equivalent.

(2) <u>American Petroleum Institute (API 1581)</u>. For aviation Filter/ Separators (F/S) at large volume, bulk storage and refuelers.

NOTE. All future references to multistage Filter/Separators are understood to have met requirements of the API 1581 or equivalent. Group and class for large volume bulk storage and group and class for refuelers.

Chapter 4 Filtration   **4.3B**

B. All filters must match the pumping pressures and flow rate in gallons per minute (gpm) of the facility (see 4.8).

C. Any individual responsible for an aviation refueling facility must assure adherence to the manufacturer's specified conditions for filter installation, maintenance, inspection, and element change-out.

4.4 Filter Types. In refueling operations, filters can be divided into two different types, single element and multistage.

A. Single-Stage or Filter Monitor. Vessels containing water-absorbent elements which will continuously remove dirt and water from aviation fuels down to a level acceptable for servicing modern aircraft. It will positively shut off the flow if the concentration of water is unacceptable (see Appendix A.5). Single elements or filter monitors will ensure (provided properly sized and maintained to manufacturer's specifications) the effluent fuel contamination shall meet current and related aviation industry standards such as Institute of Petroleum (IP) performance specifications for allowable effluent:

Total Solids	-- 0.3 mg/liter or 1.1 mg/U.S. gallon - average
	-- 0.5 mg/liter or 1.9 mg/U.S. gallon - maximum
Free Water	-- 15 ppm (parts per million) - volume
Media Migration	-- 10 fibers/liter (see Appendix A.5)

CAUTION: Design maximum operating pressures should never be exceeded on any filter system. Elements can be forced to rupture and allow unfiltered fuel into the effluent.

B. Multistage Filter/Separator. Large vessel filters are usually an F/S-type fitted with several elements. In some combination, these elements will remove dirt and water from aviation fuels down to a level acceptable for servicing modern air-craft engines (see Appendix A.5). One example of a multistage F/S type is the three-stage F/S:

(1) First-Stage Coalescer removes solids/particulates and breaks the fuel-water emulsions and coalesces the finer water molecules into larger droplets. The larger droplets drift to the bottom of the vessel and are removed during vessel sumping.

(2) Second-Stage Separators (teflon-coated metal screen) separates out remaining agglomerated water droplets.

(3) Third-Stage Monitor (Go-No-Go) monitors the fuel before leaving the vessel as effluent. If there is sufficient free water passing through the second-stage, the monitor mechanically shuts down the flow.

NOTE. The multistage F/S systems typically specify a minimum flow rate to assure the monitor stage will be effective in stopping the flow if free water is present in the fuel. If less than 25% of the system's maximum rated flow cannot be maintained at the dispensing nozzle, the manufacturer will not guarantee the monitor's shutoff performance. To prevent passing free water, this limitation must be under-stood and closely controlled. Any changes to the system; such as pump size or performance, hose size or length; requires testing to assure the flow rate is within the specified limits. By replacing the existing monitor stage with a single-stage monitor, such as a Velcon YF-61 filter housing with an ACO-51201B element, the flow rate limitation is eliminated.

NOTE. If multistage F/S units continue to be used, it is highly recommended to convert the first and second stages to elements in conformance with API 1581, Third Edition, and the third stage to qualified elements with absorbent type media (see Appendix A.5). Then, if required flow rates cannot be maintained, the absorbent media would provide clean and bright effluent or positive shutdown.

4.5 Filter Applications. There are typically three individual applications for filter types listed above.

A. First Application. Remote sites, where low volume and low flow rates (8-20 gpm) are required. The proper filter would be an aviation-type, single element absorbent monitor with spin-on design.

B. Second Application. Remote sites or fixed refueling sites/facilities where medium flow rates (20-50 gpm) are required. A proper filter would be a large volume aviation-type, single element absorbent monitor with fixed mounting design. Another appropriate application for this larger single element filter is downstream from a multistage F/S where 75 feet or more of hose is required for delivery. The exact position of this single element monitor would be as close to the nozzle as practical, provided it is bonded to the fuel system.

C. Third Application. Fixed bases where large volume storage or high volume flow rates (100 gpm plus) are required. A proper filter would be a multistage F/S. In this case, the multistage F/S would not be modified with first and second-stage elements with absorbent media. Large volume storage implies large quantities of water and coalescers allow for water to be sumped, thus prolonging the life of the elements. Alternatively acceptable would be a two-stage aviation filter/separator followed by an aviation-type (qualified) absorbent monitor.

CAUTION: Many DOI aviation managers, pilots, mechanics, and procuring officials, among others, describe aviation filters with the term "go-no-go". Prior to 1981, that term did only relate to aviation filters; however, this is no longer true. "Go-no-go" has become generic and its meaning, when used by individuals skilled in fuel quality control concepts and language, is any device that has "absorbent type media". Consequently, it is very important when ordering new or replacement filters, that individuals should state more detailed specifications in order to avoid all the NON-AVIATION unapproved "go-no-go" filters on the market.

4.6 Differential Pressure. Pressure is measured in pounds per square inch (psi). Pressure differential across a filter element is measured as psiD. By manufacturers' recommendations, absorbent monitor filters downstream of pumps capable of discharge of pressures in excess of 25 psi shall have a gauge(s) to measure differential pressure, e.g. inlet pressure (IP) minus (-) outlet pressure (OP) equals (=) psiD (IP - OP = psiD). Additionally, manufacturers recommend filter change-out when specific levels of psiD are reached.

Chapter 4 Filtration   **4.6**

NOTE. A low or near zero psiD reading may indicate the filter element is missing or has been ruptured.

4.7 <u>Filter Change-Out Criteria</u>.

    A. <u>Small Filters</u>. Small, 8-13 gpm, single element, throw-away, spin-on filters can be fitted with differential pressure gauges. These spin-on filters, commonly called "cartridges", should be replaced if there is an excess of 15 psiD; or if there is a noticeable reduction in flow rate; or after 2 years in service, which ever occurs first. This type of spin-on cartridge has a maximum operating pressure rating of 50 psi and must <u>not</u> be installed on systems that can produce higher operating pressures.

    B. <u>Single-Stage Vessels</u>. Large, 13-50 gpm, single element, fixed vessel, with replaceable filter elements have maximum operating pressures of 150 psi. These single elements should be replaced whenever there is a 15 psiD; or a noticeable reduction in flow rate; or after 2 years service, whichever occurs first.

NOTE: Aviation contracts require changing of elements every year prior to contract start.

    C. <u>Multistage Filters/Separators (F/S)</u>. Multistage F/S's have similar differential pressure (psiD) element change-out recommendations by the manufacturers.

        (1) Multistage F/S.

            (a) First- and third-stage elements must be changed at least annually.

            (b) All second-stage elements must be inspected, cleaned, tested, replaced as necessary according to manufacturer's recommendations.

            (c) The filter unit must be placarded with the date of element cleaning and/or change-out, according to D. below.

        (2) Two-Stage F/S. Manufacturer's recommendations must be followed.

    D. <u>Filter Vessel Tagging/Placarding</u>. All filter vessels shall be tagged or placarded with the following information:

        (1) F/S elements manufacturer's change-out recommendations and instructions.

        (2) Manufacturer's information regarding change-out if the F/S has been modified.

        (3) Date of element change-out.

        (4) Legibly printed name of the individual completing the change-out.

> **NOTE:** No system should ever be operated at a flow rate greater than for which the filter system is qualified or rated.

Chapter 5 Standards   **5.1**

5.1 Quality of Product. Acceptable quality of fuel will be:

A. Specifications. Compliance with the product specification for the product furnished. Fuel purchase invoices should be accompanied by an API Gravity and a representative Manufacturer's Fuel Analysis or the Manufacturer's Product Specification Sheet. These items should remain attached to the invoice.

B. Solids/Particulates. When the particulates content is more than 1.9 milligrams per gallon (1.9 mg/G) or 0.5 milligrams per liter (0.5 mg/L) as determined on a 0.8 micron filter membrane, it indicates the system is not operating properly. The use of fuels contaminated above 1.9 mg/G or 0.5 mg/L is unacceptable; the system must be shut down and a determination made as to the source of contamination. Single-stage and multistage element monitors should be selected according to the fuel type being filtered (Appendix A.5 and paragraphs 4.4 and 4.5).

(1) AVGAS. A 5-micron qualified (rated) element is the current industry standard.

(2) Jet Fuel. A 1-micron qualified (rated) element is the current industry standard.

C. Free Water. The product must not contain more than 15 parts per million (ppm) free water when tested.

D. Media Migration. Media migration is 10 fibers/liter (industry standard).

E. Recommendation. Since both micron rated sizes are typically stocked by bureaus, it is highly recommended that all single-stage element monitors be at the 1-micron rating.

5.2 Technical Requirements - Fuel Servicing Equipment.

A. Filter. Aircraft will be serviced through a single-stage element monitor or multistage F/S unit equipped with sumps and sump drain valves for manual operation. F/S units and single element monitors shall be equipped with pressure differential gauges whenever the pump is capable of exceeding 25 psi or greater (chapter 4, Filtration).

B. Nozzle Spout Screen. Nozzle spout screens will be 100-mesh or finer and readily accessible for inspection and cleaning.

> **CAUTION.** Barrel pump nozzles typically do not have screens, dust caps, or bonding cables with clips. Pilots must exercise greater vigilance when pumping from a barrel. Nozzles must be carefully inspected for dirt particulates, and barrels must always be suspect for water. Nozzle spouts must be bonded (or in direct contact with) the aircraft fuel filler port before pumping.

C. Hose. Only aviation fueling hose meeting API Bulletin 1529 specifications, specifically designed for aircraft fuel servicing shall be used.

D. <u>Meters</u>. Annually, meters will be calibrated and certified to an accuracy of plus or minus 0.3 percent. **NOTE:** This only applies to U.S. Government supplied fuel.

5.3 <u>Fixed Facility Basic Design Criteria</u>. Control of fuel contamination (and the related serious effects of flammable fuels) starts with the basics of facility design. A checklist has been prepared (see paragraph 5.3D below) to help design the basic criteria for a fixed facility. Basic criteria for fixed facilities are designed to reduce dependency in human involvement and increase dependability of the system. Items on the checklist include:

A. Storage tanks should be constructed of epoxy lined, fiberglass, or nonferrous interior materials. All aboveground storage tanks should have a light exterior color (such as a silver, aluminum, or white color).

B. Tanks should be installed with a low point sump, such as a slope of 1/4" per foot for horizontal tanks, ensuring the point of the intake suction or fixed draw pipe opening is at the high end.

C. A floating intake system should be used.

D. Liquid products should be received into tank storage through an aviation qualified filtration system.

E. Dedicated type (non-interchangeable) product unloading and receiving couplers, and industry standard product markings on system components.

F. Flex-joints should be incorporated on tank piping and other piping subject to physical stress, and screwed fittings avoided on unexposed piping.

G. Watertight, lockable tank fill caps and receiving couplers should be used.

H. Rainproof, positive pressure/vacuum type tank venting apparatus should be used.

I. The use of cadmium, zinc, (such as galvanized), or copper components that would comprise or have contact with the main fuel stream needs to be avoided. Use of their alloys, such as brass, should be avoided. Metals such as aluminum or stainless steel are most preferable from the aspect of effect on fuel properties.

J. Whenever practical, only aviation dispensing nozzles with dust caps, 100-mesh or finer spout screens, and bond cables should be used.

CAUTION: Barrel pump nozzles may not be protected by spout screens.

K. Use is recommended of adequately sized filtration units located as near as practical to the point of dispensing the product into an aircraft, which are performance qualified for aviation use under applicable industry specifications.

L. Use is recommended of a flow "shut off" (monitor) feature such as a filter equipped with aviation qualified absorbent type cartridges (such as qualified Aquacon cartridges), or at minimum, a feature such as a water detecting device in the sump of a filter separator coupled to shut down the pump or close a slug valve (such as a water detecting device in sump of F/S). Coalescer and/or separators will have one flow "shutoff" monitor in same sump.

M. Differential pressure gauges at fixed fueling facilities should be installed on all filters, and product sampling probes and couplers upstream and downstream of all filters (see Appendix A.2, Manual of Aviation Fuel Quality Control Pro-cedures for information about sampling probes and couplers).

N. Detailed fuel handling procedures unique to the facility need to be developed and training obtained on how to perform them correctly. This should include fuel contamination detection procedures via established guidelines for sampling and testing (for example; visual, calorimetric, API gravity, Aqua-Glo, gravimetric, lab analysis, etc.) The Alaska Regional Office Fuel Quality Control Specialist may be contacted for additional information/guidance relative to their fueling operations and for the conterminous 48 states, OAS Technical Services in Boise may be contacted.

O. Quality control records need to be established and maintained.

Chapter 6 Bonding   **6.1**

6.1 <u>General</u>. It is important to remove all sources of ignition in the vicinity of any fuel handling operation. Sources of ignition such as open flames, engines, ground/ airborne radar signals, etc. are covered in some detail in Appendix B, <u>Sources of Ignition</u>. Less obvious is the ignition source hazard offered by static electricity.

6.2 <u>Static Electricity</u>. Static electricity, sufficient to cause combustion of fuel vapors, can occur by the free falling of fuel liquids into tanks, flowing through a pipe, filter or hose, by pouring from one container into another, or the splashing of fuel into a fueler or aircraft during loading and fueling/defueling operations. One serious source of static electricity is the pouring of AVGAS from plastic containers into aircraft tanks. The issue of static electricity and its associated hazard relating to fuel handling operations as an ignition source is covered in more detail in Appendix B, <u>Sources of Ignition</u>.

6.3 <u>Bonding</u>. To minimize the hazard of static electricity, it is necessary to equalize the electrical charges before they build-up to a high enough potential to create a static spark. Prior to making any fueling connection to the aircraft, the fueling equipment shall be bonded to the aircraft by use of a cable, thus providing a conductive path to equalize potential between the fueling equipment and aircraft. The nozzle shall be bonded with a nozzle bond cable having a clip or plug to a metallic component of the aircraft that is metallically connected to the tank filler port. If there is no plug receptacle or means for attaching a clip, the operator shall touch the filler cap with the nozzle spout before removing the cap so as to equalize the potential between the nozzle and the filler port. The spout shall be kept in contact with the filler neck until the fueling is completed. When a funnel is used in aircraft fueling, it shall be kept in contact with the filler neck as well as the fueling nozzle spout or the supply container.

6.4 <u>Plastic</u>. Plastic funnels and containers <u>should never be used</u> in aircraft fueling. Additionally, greater potential for sparks and subsequent ignition of aviation fuels exists whenever plastic containers, or funnels, are used. These items should be avoided unless an emergency situation exists.

6.5 <u>Bonding Procedures</u>. Bonding shall be accomplished as specified in National Fire Protection Association (NFPA) #407, <u>Standard for Aircraft Fuel Servicing</u>, restated below, prior to any fuel handling operations:

    A. <u>Bonding to Aircraft.</u> Prior to making any fueling connection to the air-craft, the fueling equipment shall be bonded to the aircraft by the use of a cable, thus providing a conductive path to equalize potential between the fueling equip-ment and aircraft. The bond shall be maintained until fueling connections have been removed.

    B. <u>Overwing Refueling</u>. When fueling overwing, the nozzle shall be bonded with a nozzle bond cable having a clip or plug to a metallic component of the aircraft that is metallically connected to the tank filler port. The bond connection shall be made before the filler cap is removed. If there is no plug receptacle or means of attaching a clip, the operator shall touch the filler cap with the nozzle spout before removing the cap so as to equalize the potential between the nozzle and the filer port. The spout shall be kept in contact with the filler neck until fueling is completed.

Chapter 6 Bonding   6.6

6.6 <u>Special Considerations When Handling Fuels</u>.

    A. <u>Splashing</u>. Splashing can be minimized during the loading of a fueler by placing the end of the loading spout at, or as near as possible to, the compartment bottom. Fuel flow would be reduced until the spout end is covered with fuel. When filling large storage tanks, splashing can be minimized by slowing down the initial flow rate until the end of the tank inlet line is covered with at least two feet of fuel. Bottom filling should be employed whenever available.

    B. <u>Metal or Conductive Objects</u>. Objects such as inventory gauge tapes, sample containers and thermometers should not be suspended or lowered into a tank or fueler compartment while it is being filled. Any static charge which may be present should be given at least 20 minutes after cessation of flow to bleed off before using these devices.

6.7 <u>Other Special Considerations/Procedures</u>. Where practicable when servicing from barrels with hand-operated or power-driven pumps, those procedures outlined in paragraph 7.7C will be followed. At minimum, bonding procedures are required. Gasoline and other low flashpoint flammable liquids will not be handled in open buckets (except for surveillance quality control checks). Bonding overwing nozzles to the aircraft shall not be waived.

6.8 <u>Equipment for Bonding</u>.

    A. <u>Bonding Cables</u>. Bonding cables will be of a flexible, durable design and material.

    B. <u>Plug and Jack Assembly</u>. The plug and jack assembly and the spring clamp will be of unpainted, non-rusting metal.

    C. <u>Testing the Bonding System</u>. Annually, the bonding system (cables and connections) will be tested for electrical resistance, and periodically inspected for continuity and integrity as required by frequency of use and type of cable.

Chapter 7 Government Fueling Operations   **7.1**

7.1 <u>General</u>. Due to the often remote conditions with which DOI personnel operate, they may be called upon to conduct refueling operations of their own aircraft or another aircraft, often under extreme in-field conditions. It is these situations this particular chapter is designed to address. All safety precautions must be observed during fueling and defueling operations. Inattention on the part of those who service aircraft or handle fuels, endangers the safety of the crew, passengers and themselves as well as Government property.

NOTE: Fuel trucks shall carry sufficient petroleum product absorbent pad or materials to absorb or contain up to a 5-gallon petroleum spill. The vendor is responsible for proper disposal of all products used in the cleanup of a spill in accordance with the Environmental Protection Agency, and CFR Parts 261 and 262.

7.2 <u>Responsibility</u>.

    A. <u>Fueling Personnel</u>. Prior to beginning fueling operations, fueling personnel will check with the flight crew to determine the type, grade and quantity of fuel required.

    B. <u>Pilot/Copilot</u>. The pilot or copilot is responsible to check and assure the fuel to be placed in the aircraft is of the proper type and grade requested. In most cases it is appropriate for a flight crew member to remain with the aircraft until all fueling operations **are complete**.

7.3 <u>Personnel Training</u>. The responsible bureau shall establish and maintain a safety training program for personnel involved with aircraft refueling, as well as the individuals designated to conduct sampling and testing of fuel products. They shall be trained in the step-by-step procedures covered in this section. Emphasis shall be placed on the quality control requirements for aviation fuels (chapter 3), the sources of ignition for fire (Appendix B) and bonding (chapter 6). Any accident involving fuel, an aircraft, or a refueling vehicle <u>may</u> result in fire. Only fuelers who have completed appropriate safety training and have demonstrated their ability to refuel aircraft using the proper procedures shall be assigned to aircraft refueling operations.

7.4 <u>Vehicle Pre-Operational Checks</u>. There are two types of pre-operational checks:

    A. Refueler's mechanical and electrical systems, i.e., foot brakes, lights, airtank reservoir, tires, emergency brake, etc. (see Refuelers Operations Manual).

    B. Refueling system, i.e., pump, hose, nozzles, recirculation, emergency valve operations, tank sumping, filter vessel sumping, nozzle sample, nozzle screen, pressure-differential, etc. (see Appendix A.1 and paragraph 8.2).

7.5 <u>Sequence of Operations</u>. Refueling should require two individuals, the fueler and the pilot. A fire extinguisher should be within reach of each. Where possible, the pilot should be present to oversee the entire operation and another member of the aircraft or ground crew should man the fire extinguisher at the nozzle. After the aircraft parks, its engines are shut down and/or the rotor blades secured; the refueling operation sequence can start. The procedures must be done in the sequence described below. When closed-circuit refueling is being done from the refueler, procedures must be supplemented with those in paragraph 7.6F.

A   Aircraft Checking. The interior of the aircraft must be checked. No one should be on board during refueling unless an aircrew member must be on board to monitor the quantity of fuel to be loaded.

B.   Refueler Positioning. The refueler must be driven into position in front of the aircraft. It should not be driven directly toward the aircraft because brake failure could cause a serious accident.

(1) Minimum distances. A distance of at least 10 feet should be kept between the refueler and the aircraft. There must be at least 10 feet between the refueler and rotor blades of a helicopter. A distance of at least 20 feet should be kept between the exhaust pipe of the pump engine refueler and the aircraft fill port.

(2) Refueler path. The refueler should be parked so that there is a clear and open path to drive it away from the aircraft in an emergency. A tank trailer should not be detached from its tractor when refueling an aircraft. The tractor must be ready to pull the trailer away from the aircraft if the necessary.

(3) Ground guides. If possible, the refueler should be driven into position without backing. If the refueler must be backed toward the aircraft, the truck must be brought to a full stop 20 to 25 feet away from the aircraft and/or its rotor blades. Another individual should act as a ground guide and his/her signals followed to guide the final backing approach until the refueler is stopped at the proper distance from the aircraft and its fill port and vent.

(4) Parking. The refueler's engine (unless it powers the pump) must be stopped and the brake set. Tires of the refueler, and if appropriate, the aircraft, should be chocked.

(5) Refueler must be bonded to the aircraft.

C.   Fuel Check. Refueler product placards must be checked to make sure it is the right type and grade for the aircraft.

D.   Fire Extinguishers. The refueler fire extinguishers must be placed by the fueler in a position where they will not be in the fueler's way and where they are not likely to be engulfed if a fire should start.

E.   Bonding Nozzle to Aircraft. The nozzle must be bonded to the aircraft before the dust cap is taken off the nozzle. If the aircraft has a receiver for the bond plug, it should be used. If not, the alligator clip must be attached to a bare metal part of the aircraft.

F.   Open Fill Port/Closed Circuit Refueling (CCR). After the fill port is opened, the nozzle dust cap must be removed. If an open-port nozzle or the closed circuit refueling (CCR) nozzle adapter is being used, the nozzle well must be put down into the port. The nozzle should not be opened until it is inside the fill port. If the CCR nozzle is being used, the nozzle needs to be mated into the fill port. If they will not latch together, dirt may have gotten in the fill port or on the nozzle. The fill port would need to be wiped out and the nozzle cleaned before mating the two together. Fueling operations should not be attempted with a leaking nozzle attachment.

G. Fuel Delivery. The procedures for refueling depend on the type of refueling to be conducted, open-port, closed circuit, underwing, etc. The aircraft operator's manual should be consulted for specific guidance.

7.6 Fuel Dispensing Operations.

A. General. Many common elements or cautions identified for safety during fuel handling, and for all fueling operations, are common regardless of the equipment or method utilized to dispense fuels. These common elements are described below, with specific issues of a particular system or method identified under separate heading. NOTE: It is highly recommended that the pilot be present to personally ensure the proper type, grade and quality of fuel is dispensed into each aircraft.

(1) Personnel dispensing fuels shall ensure the refueler, fixed system, or container contains the correct type and grade of fuel required.

(2) NO SMOKING signs shall be prominently displayed and observed.

(3) Fueling operations shall not be conducted within a building nor within 50 feet of a building.

(4) "HOT REFUELING" (refueling with the engines running) shall **ONLY** be conducted when a closed-circuit system (CCS) is present on both the pumping and receiving equipment.

(5) Fueling personnel shall not carry matches or lighters on their person during fuel handling operations.

(6) Inadvertent contamination of clothing with fuel during fuel handling operations is common AND VERY HAZARDOUS (refer to Appendix A, SOURCES OF IGNITION for more detailed information on your individual safety).

(a) Recent documented studies indicate that no single type fabric currently in use retains an advantage for less static buildup than any other. All type fabrics tested, i.e., 100% cotton, cotton/polyester, and NOMEX, all produced voltages in excess of that required for fuel/air mixture (vapor) ignition when separated from each other or removed from the body.

(b) The factor of static electricity in clothing becomes most critical when fuel saturated garments are removed from the individual. Therefore, the following procedures will be adhered to when removing clothing due to accidental saturation by any type of aviation fuel.

(i) Eliminate static charge potential by placing both hands on the bonded system for a few seconds. This will help considerably but will not reduce all static electrical buildup.

(ii) The fuel-soaked area should be thoroughly doused with water.

(iii) Another individual should be present with a fire extinguisher prior to removal of any garment.

(iv) Static electricity buildup in clothing is a dangerous hazard which must be dealt with efficiently if fire and resulting burns are to be avoided.

(7) When required, only explosion-proof flashlights or radios should be used.

(8) The aircraft and refueling equipment shall be properly bonded before refueling operations begin. Before opening aircraft filler cap(s), the nozzle bonding plug/alligator clip shall be connected to the aircraft to equalize static discharge potential between the fuel container/vehicle/etc. and the aircraft. Chapter 6, **BONDING** contains more detailed information on individual safety.

(9) The fuel hose should not be allowed to drape over the aircraft wings trailing edge.

(10) The fuel hose should not be "dragged" over an aircraft leading edge.

(11) A simple rubber shower mat may be used to provide protection for wing leading edges during fueling operations.

(12) Dispensing nozzles will not be utilized if they have "notched" handles (those that can be blocked open and left unattended during refueling). If such notched fuel nozzles are discovered, they shall immediately be removed from service.

(13) Into-aircraft nozzles shall never be blocked or wedged open while dispensing fuel.

(14) Fuel nozzles are not to be dragged across the surface as contaminants may become lodged within the nozzle.

(15) All fuel nozzles (with the exception of barrel hand pump nozzles) shall be equipped with screens and dust caps. All dust caps shall be in place over the exposed nozzle end when not in use.

(16) The fueler, and the pilot, should check to ensure that nothing was inadvertently left on the wings or around the moving parts of the engine, flaps, ailerons, etc., and that all bonding cables are properly stowed before starting engines or moving the aircraft.

(17) Leaking or otherwise defective pumping equipment, plumbing, hoses, nozzles, bonding cables, etc., shall be repaired before further use.

Chapter 7 Government Fueling Operations   7.6B

B. <u>Portable Storage Facilities/Containers</u>. Many of the requirements, guidelines and precautions already identified in this section will apply to portable storage facilities as well. Refueling from barrels and containers should be avoided whenever possible and the use of portable rollagons and bladders is encouraged. Project supervisors should consider the advantages of using portable, collapsible rubber containers, when available. In remote sites, where it is necessary to fuel from drums or cans, extra precautions must be taken to eliminate the hazards of contamination and the generation of static electricity (refer Appendix B, <u>Sources of Ignition</u>). Additionally, the following information/pre-cautions should be noted when utilizing portable/remote site containers, e.g. 55-gallon barrels, rubber bladders, rollagons, etc.

C. **Barrel Fuel**. **NOTE**: Use of barrel fuel is limited to Alaska only.

(1) Procurement. Whenever possible, barrel fuel should be purchased through OAS in Anchorage, AK. This process will help ensure that clean, dry (water-free) fuel of the proper type and grade is provided by the fuel vendor and is contained in <u>NEW</u> (or reconditioned) 55-gallon barrels.

(2) Barrel Labeling. Each barrel <u>must</u> be labeled or stenciled indicating the product it contains and date it was filled.

(3) Storage. Whenever barrels are stored, they must be stored on the side, off the ground with the bungs laterally (below the fluid level). If a storage site contains more than one grade/type of fuel, such as AVGAS and Jet Fuel, the barrels must be separated by fuel type -- all Jet Fuel barrels in one area and all AVGAS barrels in another area, separated by a minimum of six feet.

(4) Inspection. The pilot of an aircraft being refueled from any barrel is personally responsible for verifying that fuel to be pumped into the aircraft <u>is</u> the proper type and grade and is free from water, dirt or other contaminants.

(5) Pumping. All fuel, regardless of type and grade, must be pumped through a pump and filter that has <u>not</u> been used to pump another type of fuel that would contaminate it. <u>Example</u>: Refueling a piston-engine aircraft requiring 100LL AVGAS through a pump and filter previously used to pump Jet Fuel would very likely cause engine failure and result in an accident. (<u>CAUTION</u>: Turbine engines can operate for a period of time on AVGAS; gas engines will not operate on Jet Fuel or AVGAS commingled with Jet Fuel.)

(6) Re-using Barrels. Barrels to be refilled with a different type and/or grade of fuel shall first be cleaned and flushed with the new product. All old markings and labeling must be removed or completely obliterated; the barrel then must be marked and/or labeled to comply with paragraph (2) above, <u>Barrel Labeling</u>.

(7) Bonding is as important in these remote site refueling operations as any other time and should be closely adhered to (chapter 6).

D. <u>Fixed Refueling Sites</u>. Interior bureaus operate fixed refueling sites (paragraphs 5.3 and 5.4). Appropriate standards, procedures, safety precautions, etc. identified within this Handbook shall be adhered to for all such DOI refueling activities. Additionally:

(1) Bureaus shall designate and appropriately train an individual to oversee and administer local/unit fixed refueling sites. Bureaus are responsible to:

(a) Develop an operating procedure for administration of such site.

(b) Maintain refueling site records for fuels received, stored, and dispensed.

(c) Conduct annual site and repetitive routine inspection.

(2) The OAS Alaska Regional Office Fuels Quality Control Specialist shall be contacted for assistance as applicable, and OAS Division of Technical Services, Boise for the conterminous 48 states.

(a) New fixed or portable temporary refueling sites are proposed to be constructed.

(b) Existing portable or fixed refueling sites are suspect as to adherence to Interior standards identified within this Handbook.

(c) Questions regarding fuels transportation, storage, handling or testing.

E. Safety. A safety program shall consist of at least the following:

(1) Fueling operations being conducted with adequately trained personnel.

(2) Proper bonding of fuel servicing equipment and aircraft.

(3) Fire extinguisher(s) must be suitable, operable and located immediately available to the refueling operations.

(4) NO SMOKING signs must be posted. (No smoking or open flame within 50 feet radially of servicing points).

(5) Spills must be avoided and cleaned up immediately should they occur (paragraph 1.5).

(6) Fuel saturated clothing must be carefully removed to avoid static discharge (paragraph 7.7A(6)(c)).

7.7 Follow-up Emergency Fire and Rescue Procedures. After a fire or emergency involving aviation fuels, several follow-up actions must be accomplished. These are described below.

A. Refueling Site Closure. The extent to which the refueling point must be closed depends on the nature and type of fire or emergency and the extent of the damage. If a fuel spill occurred, the area must be roped off until the spill is cleaned up.

B. Damage Assessment. The extent of damage shall be reported to the bureau Safety Manager and the nearest OAS Area/Regional office.

C. <u>Fuel Sampling</u>. Under no conditions should aviation fuel that has been contaminated by fire extinguishing agents or dirt be used until it has been sampled and tested by a laboratory.

D. <u>Fuel Spill Cleanup</u>. Spilled fuel should not be flushed into sewers, drains, or natural waterways. The spill area should be immediately diked with earth containment or fuel absorbent pads.

7.8 <u>Fire Extinguisher Requirements</u>. As a minimum, one 100-pound or two 30-pound fire extinguisher(s) with an NFPA BC rating will be immediately available during all refueling/defueling operations. Where specific requirements are not identified, individuals responsible for overall safety of refueling operations will exercise good judgment when conducting these activities.

Chapter 8 Inspections   8.1

8.1 <u>General</u>. Every possible precaution must be taken to maintain quality assurance. The major items of an operational nature which should be checked and maintained on a daily, weekly, monthly and demand basis are covered in Figures 8-1 and 8-2.

NOTE. To properly accomplish a total fuel system inspection, it will be necessary to recirculate fuel. The amount depends on size and volume of the fuel system.

8.2 <u>Daily Inspections or Prior to Use (All Filter Systems)</u>.

    A. <u>Storage Facility</u>.

        (1) Tanks. The bottom of storage tanks shall be checked for gross water, and/or a visual test with a water-finding paste conducted.

        (2) Filter. A sample shall be drawn from the storage facility filter sump and nozzle. The sample will be collected in a clean, clear, one-quart bottle or jar and swirled to generate a vortex in the container. Water and dirt become readily apparent in this vortex of fuel. Any visual water, dirt or filter fibers is not acceptable and the filter system should be inspected immediately (details in chapter 4).

    B. <u>Refueler</u>.

        (1) Tanks. Fuel handler shall check for and remove any gross water from refueler tanks. A water check shall also be performed after every refilling of the refueler, washing of the equipment, and after a heavy rain or snow storm.

        (2) Filters. All installed filter vessels (filter/separators and/or single-element monitors) shall be checked, and all water and contaminants drained. After each refilling of the refueler, as well as prior to use each day, gross water found in a monitor vessel requires an immediate filter system inspection (see chapter 4 for details).

    C. <u>Filter Vessel Drains.</u> Check all filters or separators and large volume single element monitor vessels manual water drains for water and other contaminants after each receipt of fuel, as well as on a daily basis. Any accumulation of water must be drawn off. If any gross water is found in large single element monitor vessels, an inspection of tank product and filter is immediately required.

    D. <u>Differential Pressure</u>. All refueler, fixed single element monitors and filter/separator (F/S) differential pressures must be checked and recorded while under full flow conditions. A graph-type log may be used in plotting daily differential pressure.

NOTE. Any sudden change or decrease in pressure differential (psiD) may indicate a ruptured filter (chapter 4).

FILTER/DIFFERENTIAL RECORD - Daily Log

NOTE ANY SERVICES TO FILTERS ON REVERSE SIDE									
Equipment Type/No._____Grade/Type Fuel									
Filter/Separator Type_____S/N									
Date	Inlet Pressure	Outlet Pressure	Differential	Initials	Date	Inlet Pressure	Outlet Pressure	Differential	Initials

Figure 8-1 (sample format)

E. <u>Bonding Plugs/Clips</u>. Bonding plugs/clips must be checked to ensure they are in place and not worn or damaged so as to be unserviceable.

F. <u>Refueler Plumbing</u>. Refueler and storage facilities, pumps, valves, hoses, hose couplings, pipe, plumbing, etc., must be visually inspected for leaks on a daily basis.

G. <u>Nozzle Screens</u>. Nozzle spout screens must be checked and cleaned. If breaks are found, screens need to be replaced.

H. <u>Dust Caps</u>. Dust caps must be checked to assure that they are in place.

8.3 <u>Weekly Inspections</u>

A. <u>Hoses</u>. All hoses need to be checked for abrasions, separations or soft spots. Weak hoses should be replaced.

B. <u>Fire Extinguishers</u> All fire extinguishers must be inspected for broken seals, proper pressure and recharge date; and recharged as necessary.

C. <u>Covers Gaskets and Vents</u>. The condition of covers, gaskets and vents must be checked.

8.4 <u>Monthly Inspections</u>. See Appendix A.2 and paragraph 5.1C.

A. <u>Bonding Cables</u>. The condition of static bonding cables clips, plugs, etc., should be checked.

B. <u>Refuelers and Fueling Facilities</u>. Refuelers and fueling facilities must be checked for general condition, safety and appearance. Figure 8.2 is a Facilities Inspection Log.

C. <u>Millipore Sample</u>. Each large volume tank and/or refueler should be checked once a month during the period of use with a Millipore Sampling Kit or equivalent. Large volume tanks and/or refuelers should be designed and construction with appropriate sampling taps <u>upstream</u> and <u>downstream</u> of the filter vessel.

Bureaus may elect to perform a calorimetric first, and later a gravimetric for laboratory analysis when the calorimetric indicates a signification shift (Appendix A.2 and paragraph 5.1B).

   D. Aqua-Glo. Each large volume tank and/or refueler (equipped with Millipore sampling taps) should be checked with an Aqua-Glo or equivalent tester to determine free water parts per million (ppm) in effluent (Appendix A.2 and paragraph 5.1C).

8.5 Annual Inspections. Refueler bonding cable continuity should be checked with a voltage ohmmeter prior to beginning seasonal operations, but not less than annually.

8.6 On-Site Inspection. On-site inspection and sampling of remote site fuel facilities is essential in assuring fuel quality at receipt and/or prior to dispensing into aircraft. Bureaus having remote site fueling activities should designate bureau personnel to conduct this activity. When necessary to assure safety of fuels, bureaus may request contract pilots to conduct such remote site inspections as may be necessary.

8.7 Alaska Region Operational Requirements. The remoteness of some fuel sites within the state of Alaska necessitates varying operational requirements. To facilitate these requirements, the Alaska Regional Office of the Office of Aircraft Services has published two Operational Procedures Memorandums (OPMs) entitled Fuel Procurement Services and Fuel Quality Control/Fuel Site Inspection. These are for DOI aviation operations within Alaska only.

   A. OAS Responsibility. Fuel orders facilitated by OAS as a support service for bureaus are most often filled by the Defense Fuel Contracting Office - Alaska (DFSC-AK). DFCO-AK fuel provides a "measure" of quality control at point-of-origin, and in some cases, bulk transfer sites (paragraph 10.3).

   B. Bureau Responsibility. Ensuring that aviation fuels received as ordered and meet quality standard is the responsibility of the requesting bureau who physically receives and takes possession at delivery storage location or into-aircraft transfer site. This responsibility includes assuring through visual checks, tests, and inspections by persons trained in basic fuel handling procedures, that the fuel ordered is of the proper type, grade, and quality prior to acceptance for delivery.

8.8 Bureaus Purchase of Bulk Fuel. Bureaus purchasing bulk fuel directly with a commercial vendor should require the vendor to provide the fuel manufacturer's Fuel Analysis Report or Product Specification Sheet. This report should be a condition of the procurement action and be presented to the bureau with the invoice at the time of delivery. Fuel accepted without either of these two reports have the potential of being a contaminated or commingled product.

8.9 Remote On-Site Fuel Tests.

   A. Clean/Clear and Bright. A clean/clear and bright check (Appendix A.2).

   B. Water Test. A test for gross water with water-finding paste must also be performed (chapter 3 and Appendix C). **NOTE.** A strong explosion-proof flashlight can greatly assist in locating water on the dark bottom of barrels.

C. <u>Filters</u>. The filter system must be inspected for presence of an element and change-out date within limits (paragraph 4.7D).

D. <u>Prior to Pumping Into Aircraft</u>. Prior to pumping remote site fuel into aircraft, a nozzle sample needs to be collected and another "clean/clear and bright test" conducted.

NOTE. If system is pressurized and can be recirculated, the psiD at full flow rate must be noted. High psiD (above manufacturer's recommendations) or a reduced fuel flow rate are indications of gross water/particulates contamination. A "0" psiD may indicate improperly installed or ruptured filter within the vessel.

E. <u>Fuel Nozzle Screens</u>. Fuel nozzle spout screens should be inspected and cleaned prior to use.

NOTE. Common barrel hand pumps which include hose and nozzle <u>do not</u> have a spout screen. Throat of nozzle must be inspected for cleanliness prior to pumping fuel.

8.10 <u>Assistance</u>. Assistance in the development of inspection and testing procedures for remote and fixed facility sites is available from the OAS Alaska Regional Office, or the Division of Technical Services, OAS, Boise upon request.

8.11 <u>Fuel Sampling Kit</u>. Fuel sampling equipment to facilitate collecting, testing, and transportation for laboratory analysis of sampled fuels is available from OAS Alaska Regional Office.

NOTE. Routing fuel samples commercially requires full compliance to DOT Hazard Materials Regulations (49 CFR Part 170 - 175). If fuel can be sent by DOI Fleet/ Contract/Rental Aircraft, then the requirements of 351 DM 1, <u>Aviation Transportation of Hazardous Materials Handbook</u> shall be complied with.

8.12 <u>Fuel Lock Out - Tag Out (Government Owned Operated and Controlled)</u>. If point-of-origin quality control (<u>Fuel Analysis Report</u> or <u>Product Specification Sheet</u>) cannot be verified, and no on-site testing can be accomplished, the fuel should be physically secured (lock out) and temporarily marked (tag out) to insure it is not used until such time as the steps listed in paragraph 8.10A-E, as appropriate, can be performed.

AIRCRAFT FUEL FACILITY INSPECTION LOG

Facility _____ Grade of Fuel _____ Month _____

				EQUIPMENT INSPECTIONS					
Date	Water (Daily)	Diff. Pressure (Daily)	Leaks (Daily)	Hoses Nozzles Screens (Daily)	Strainers (Weekly)	Fire Exting. (Weekly)	Pumps & Motors (Monthly)	Valves (Monthly)	Bonding & Grounding Monthly
1									
2									
3									

Figure 8-2 (sample format)
Each space must bear the appropriate remark and/or the initials of the inspector.

9.1 <u>General</u>. Provisions established herein are applicable for the reporting and investigation of any fuel contamination problems experienced by DOI bureaus. Included are fuels supplied by OAS-provided into-aircraft service contractors, bureau purchased fuel and into-aircraft service received at commercial fueling facilities.

9.2 <u>Notification</u>. OAS will be notified immediately by the most expeditious means available when a fuel contamination incident has occurred. Form OAS-34 is to be used for the written follow-up report.

9.3 <u>Investigation</u>. Personnel designated by the bureau will have the primary investigative authority in all fuel contamination incidents resulting from bureau direct purchase. OAS will be the primary authority for fuel provided by into-aircraft services contractors, fuel purchased and supplied to a bureau by OAS, and into-aircraft delivery at commercial facilities. OAS will provide technical expertise within the Alaska Region, where requested.

9.4 <u>Follow-up Actions</u>. On discovery of fuel contamination, the following actions shall be taken.

    A. <u>Notification of Pilots</u>. All pilots who fueled from the contaminated source must be <u>immediately</u> notified of the contamination.

    B. <u>Grounding Aircraft</u>. When required, all aircraft fueled from a known contaminated source shall be grounded, i.e., not scheduled for flight until re-lease is coordinated with the OAS Alaska Region Fuel Quality Control Specialist, or the Technical Specialist, Division of Technical Services, OAS, Boise.

    C. <u>Notification of Bureau</u>. Bureau management shall be notified immediately of the contamination problem, as well as commercial management when applicable.

    D. <u>Identification</u>. The vendor providing the fuel must be identified, with the batch and source of the contaminated fuel isolated.

    E. <u>Isolation</u>. Where appropriate and when practical, the batch and source of contaminated fuel must be isolated and placed in secured quarantine ("lock out-tag out") immediately after the discovery of contamination.

Chapter 10 U. S. Department of Defense (DOD) Fuel Service Contracting   **10.1**

10.1 <u>General</u>. U.S. Department of Defense (DOD) fuels are ordered for bulk delivery to OAS or other DOI aviation facilities within Alaska, and applicable locations in the conterminous U.S.

10.2 <u>Policy</u>. Whenever possible, OAS will contract with the U.S. Department of Defense Fuel Supply Center (DFSC) for delivery of aviation fuels to bureau fixed base locations and/or remote sites. These contracts may be for:

    A. Delivery and direct into-aircraft services,

    B. Delivery and transfer into DOI owned, leased, or otherwise maintained storage tanks,

    C. Delivery and transfer into a commercial facilities storage tank for later commercial operator deliveries to DOI owned or contracted storage tanks or refuelers.

10.3 <u>Defense Fuel Supply Centers (DFSCs)</u>. These DFSCs are guided by the <u>Military Standardization Handbook - Quality Surveillance for Fuels</u>, MIL-HBK-200G, July 1, 1987. This military handbook provides instruction and minimum procedures to be utilized by the military services and Defense Logistic Agency (DLA) in quality surveillance of U.S. Government owned aviation fuels.

10.4 <u>Inspection of DFSC Delivered Fuels</u>. OAS <u>does not</u> perform quality control inspections of DFSC-AK contracted fuel prior to or during time of delivery. However, OAS <u>does</u> perform on a random basis minimum quality control surveillance of these DFSC-AK delivered fuels at selected locations. These inspections typically review type and grade of fuel, identified through records and placards with DFSC codes and dates; and the clear/clean and bright test. Suspect fuel may be sampled and presented to DFSCs laboratory for product specification and particulate quantities testing (mg/L).

Chapter 11 Inventories and Reporting of Government-owned Aviation Fuels   **11.1**

11.1 <u>Form OAS-59</u>. Any movement of fuel into or out of storage, including issues to aircraft, bulk transfers to other tanks or sites, or receipt of fuel from vendors or delivery agents, must be recorded sequentially, in order, on a Form OAS-59 for:

    A. Each location, including remote site.

    B. Each tank, bladder, drum, or other storage container. (Tank(s) should be identified by number.)

    C. Each <u>product</u> type/grade.

11.2 <u>Delivery</u>. At the time of fuel delivery into storage, the following information must be recorded on the OAS-59 already set up for that storage container on the next available line:

    A. Date of delivery.

    B. Vendor company name and invoice or delivery ticket number.

    C. Quantity, in whole gallons, delivered into the storage container.

    D. Name and phone number of the DOI employee or agent receiving the fuel and recording the receipt.

The vendor's invoice or delivery ticket is to be signed and dated by the DOI employee receiving the delivery and mailed immediately to OAS Procurement.

11.3 <u>Physical Inventories, Recordkeeping and Mailing to OAS</u>. Complete records of receipts, issues and physical inventory measurements must be maintained for each site (as defined at 11.1 above), regardless of whether the site operates year around or seasonally.

    A. <u>Reporting during Operating Season</u>.

        (1) All inventory changes, including deliveries, issues, and transfers; and month-end physical inventory measurements must be recorded on Form OAS-59 and sent to OAS Procurement.

        (2) Physical inventory record lines must include date, the words "physical inventory," measured gallons on hand, and name and phone number of person taking the inventory, legibly written or printed. The entry must be on the next available line of Form OAS-59, in sequential order.

    B. <u>Reporting at Beginning and End of Season</u>.

        (1) On the day a seasonal site is opened for the year, a physical inventory must be taken before any deliveries are received or any issues are made. This inventory must be recorded but need not be mailed immediately to OAS; the Form OAS-59 may be used to record issues and deliveries subsequent to the physical inventory.

(2) On the day a site is closed for the season, the physical inventory is to be taken and recorded as the last entry on the Form OAS-59, the form itself pulled, copies and mailed to OAS Procurement.

C. <u>Retention of Records</u>. Copies of all Form OAS-59s should be kept at the facility site for a minimum of 12 months.

11.4 <u>Inventory Technique</u>.

A. Only trained personnel shall be used.

B. Only "industry standard" metal inventory gauging tape and bob shall be used.

C. Industry standard gauging paste shall be used.

D. Gross "water-finding" paste shall be used during all inventories.

BIBLIOGRAPHY

A.1 Air Transportation Association of America (ATA) Products Standards for Jet Fuel. ATA specification No. 103, January 15, 1989.

A.2 Manual of Aviation Fuel Quality Control Procedures. American Society for Testing and Materials Manual Service: MNL 5, Editor Rick Waite, 1989.

A.3 Handbook of Aviation Fuel Properties. American Petroleum Institute (API), C.R.C. Report # 530, 3rd Printing, May 1988.

A.4 Specifications and Qualification Procedures for Aviation Jet Fuel Filter Separators (F/S). American Petroleum Institute Bulletin 1581, 3rd Edition, May 1989.

A.5 Specifications and Qualification Procedures - Aviation Fuel Filter Monitor with Absorbent Type Elements. Institute of Petroleum, June 1987.

A.6 Aviation Fuel Quality Control Manual. Chevron U.S.A. Inc.

A.7 NASA Technical Memorandum, "An Evaluation of the Relative Fire Hazards of Jet A and Jet B For Commercial Flight", by Robert R. Hibbard and Paul T. Hacker, Lewis Research Center, Cleveland, Ohio, Oct. 1973.

A.8 DOT/FAA Advisory Circular, AC No. 00-34A, date: 7-29-74, Subject: Aircraft Ground Handling and Servicing.

A.9 DOT/FAA Advisory Circular, AC No. 91-13C, date: 7-24-79, Subject: Cold Weather Operations of Aircraft.

A.10 DOT/FAA Advisory Circular, AC No. 150/5230-4, Change 2, Subject: Change 2 to Aircraft Fuel Storage Handling and Dispensing on Airports.

A.11 DOT/FAA Advisory Circular, AC No. 20-113, date: 10-22-81, Subject: Pilot Precautions and Procedures to be Taken in Preventing Aircraft Reciprocating Engine Induction System and Fuel System Icing Problems.

A.12 Gammon Technical Products Inc., catalog of Equipment for Handling and Testing Aviation Fuels. Petroleum Equipment Institute (PEI), distributor updated Bulletin(s).

A.13 National Fire Protection Association (NFPA) No. 407, Standard for Aircraft Fuel Servicing, 1990.

A.14 National Safety Council Aviation Ground Operation. 4th Edition, 1988.

A.15 Aviation Fueling Hose. American Petroleum Institute Bulletin 1529, 4th Edition, December 1989.

A.16 S P C C Plans. Environmental Protection Agency. October 1984.

A.17 "Are You Subject to S P C C Regulations". Environmental Protection Agency, Region 10, Alaska. May 1992.

A.18 "Title 18 AAC Chapter 15". Alaska Department of Environmental Conservation.

A.19 "Airport Equipment Marking for Fuel Identification." API Bulletin 1542, 5 Edition. January 1991.

A.20 "Remaining Professional". A fact sheet by Northland Enterprises, Inc. 1991. (Previously titled, "Avoiding Service Station Mentality". NEI, Anchorage, AK. 1993.

SOURCES OF IGNITION

B.1 **PROPERTIES OF FUELS**. How a fuel ignites depends on its physical properties. The properties of aviation and turbine fuels that relate to ease of ignition are flash point, flammability limits, vapor pressure, autoignition temperature, distillation range, and electrostatic susceptibility. These properties are charted in Table B-1.

Table B-1. Properties of Aviation Fuels

Property	Gasoline	Kerosene grades		Blends of gasoline and kerosene
	AVGAS	JET A, JP-5, JP-6	JET A-1, JP-8	JET B, JP-4
Flash Point (By Closed-Cup Method at Sea Level)	-50°F	+95° to +145°F		-10°to +30°F
Flash Point (By Air Saturation Method)	-75° to -85°F	None		-60°F
Flammability Limits Lower Limit Upper Limit Temp Range for Flam Mixtures	1.4% 7.6% -50° to +30°F	0.6% 4.9% +95° to +165°F		0.8% 5.6% -10° to +100°F
Vapor Pressure ASTM D 323	5.5 to 7.0 lb/ sq in	0.1 lb/sq in		2.0 to 3.0 lb/ sq in
Autoignition Temperature	+825° to +960°F	+440° to +475°F		+470° to 480°F
Freeze Point	-76°F	-40°F -58°F		-60°F
Boiling Points Initial End	110°F 325°F	325°F 450°F		135°F 485°F
Pool Rate of Flame Spread*	700 to 800 ft per min	100 ft per min or less		700 to 800 ft per min
*In mist form, rate of flame spread in all fuels is very rapid.				

B.2 **STATIC ELECTRICITY**

A. Nature of Static Electricity. Static electricity is formed when two unlike materials touch or rub; electrons are exchanged or redistributed between the two materials at the point or surface where they touch. This exchange of electrons causes unlike, but equal, charges on the two materials, and these charges attract each other as they seek electrical balance. It takes energy to separate the two surfaces because the force of electrical attraction is opposed. Since energy is never lost, the energy used to separate the attracting surfaces reappears as an increase in the electrical tension or voltage between the two surfaces. If a surface that has such a charge is a conductor and if there is a conductive pathway through which the charge can move, the charge will follow the path and leak away as it tries to find an unlike charge to balance it. If the surface that has such a charge is a nonconductor (insulator), the charge is trapped. The same sort of trapping of a charge happens when the charge is on a conductor that touches only nonconductors, because in this situation there is no path through which the charge can leak away. Equal but unlike static charges will stay as close as possible to each other. If the attraction between them is strong enough, the charge from one surface may jump the gap to the other surface in its search for equilibrium. This impulsive discharge of electricity results in a spark, and static sparking is a serious fire danger to refueling operations.

B. Safety Measures. The charges on different materials can be equalized by connecting them with a conductor (bonding) thus significantly reducing sparking potential from static electricity. AVGAS must not be placed in plastic containers, nor plastic funnels used. The level of static electricity build-up has sufficient potential to be an ignition source when AVGAS is poured from the plastic container. Bonding is also very difficult without the proper equipment.

C. Bonding. Bonding is the process through which two conductive objects are connected to lessen their potential differences. Bonding does not dissipate the static electricity. It equalizes the charges on two unlike objects (an aircraft and a refueling nozzle) in order to preclude arcing, in the presence of flammable vapors, as the two objects are joined. A nozzle-to-aircraft bond is required. This bond is made before the nozzle dust cap or gas tank cap is removed so that if there is a spark, it will occur before fuel vapor is present. For the same reason, the nozzle bond must not be disconnected until refueling is completed and the gas tank cap and nozzle dust cap have been replaced. Then if a spark occurs, only small amounts of fuel vapor should be present, probably not enough to support combustion.

B.3 **OTHER SOURCES OF IGNITION**

A. Engines. Operating aircraft, vehicle, and equipment engines generate heat by burning fuel. They also generate static electricity because of friction between their moving parts.

(1) Dangers. The engine heat of an idling aircraft turbine engine is in the autoignition range of JP-4. Poorly maintained vehicle engines and/or exhaust/flame arrestor systems may backfire or discharge sparks.

(2) <u>Safety Measures</u>. An aircraft must not be refueled until its engines are shut down, except as allowed under closed-circuit refueling described in chapter 4. Restrict vehicle access to the refueling area. Only those vehicles actually involved in servicing aircraft are allowed to come within 50 feet of the refueling operation. Vehicles used in and around refueling areas must be maintained to a high standard.

B. <u>Electrical Circuits</u>. When electricity is flowing through a circuit, it can jump a small break or defect in the circuit by arcing. An electrical arc is simply a continuous flow of sparks between two points.

(1) <u>Dangers</u>. The danger from arcing is the same or greater than from a spark. An arc usually generates more heat than a single spark.

(2) <u>Safety Measures</u>. Work is not allowed to be done on an aircraft's batteries while the aircraft is being refueled. Batteries should not be changed/ replaced; and battery chargers should not be connected, used, or disconnected during refueling. Aircraft radios may operate to receive messages during refueling, but radio transmission from the aircraft being refueled is not allowed because of the danger of arcing. Flashlights are not to be used within 50 feet of the refueling operation unless they are the approved explosion-proof type. Electrically powered tools are not to be used in the refueling area. The electrical circuits of vehicles used in refueling operations must be maintained in top condition to prevent short circuits around defects.

C. <u>Radar</u>. The beam of high-frequency radar equipment can ignite a flammable vapor-air mixture. It can ignite the mixture by inducing heat in solid materials in the path of the beam or by intensifying an existing electrical charge or stray current to the point where it will arc or discharge as a spark.

(1) <u>Dangers</u>. The degree of danger depends on the peak power output of the radar unit. Some types of radar are more dangerous than others as sources of ignition.

(2) <u>Safety Measures</u>. Safety measures must be taken when using airborne weather-mapping radar, airborne surveillance radar, airfield surface-detection radar, and airfield approach and traffic control radar. They are described below.

➤**Airborne weather-mapping radar**. A weather-mapping radar unit mounted in an aircraft must be shut down before and during refueling of the aircraft.

➤**Airborne surveillance radar**. Airborne surveillance units must be shut down before the aircraft approaches within 300 feet of a refueling or fuel storage area.

➤**Airfield surface-detection radar**. An aircraft must not be fueled nor aviation fuel stored within 100 feet of the antenna of an airfield surface-detection radar.

➤**Airfield approach and traffic control radar.** An aircraft must not be fueled nor aviation fuel stored within 300 feet of the antenna of an airfield approach and traffic control radar.

D. <u>Open Flames</u>. The danger of any open flame is that it will ignite fuel or a flammable vapor-air mixture. No open flame, open-flame device, or lighted smoking materials are allowed within 50 feet of an aircraft refueling operation. Personnel who refuel aircraft may not carry lighters or matches on their persons and must not allow anyone else to carry a lighter or matches within 50 feet of an aircraft that is being refueled. Use of exposed-flame heaters, welding or cutting torches, and flare pots within 50 feet of refueling operations is forbidden.

E. <u>Tools and Equipment</u>. Drills, buffers, grinding machines, and similar tools are likely to throw off sparks when used on metal. Photographic flashbulbs and electronic flash devices may also cause sparks. No metalworking tools are allowed to be used within 50 feet of an aircraft being refueled. Flashbulbs or electronic flash devices are not to be used within 10 feet of refueling equipment or the fill port or fuel tank vents of aircraft.

F. <u>Sparks from Vehicles</u>. A vehicle may pick up a static charge from two sources. One source is movement (unlike materials rubbing). The other source is the charge that spreads to the vehicle as its fuel or cargo tanks are filled. Chapter 6, <u>Bonding</u>, outlines safety measures to be taken.

G. <u>Sparks from Personnel and Clothing</u>. The human body conducts electricity. In a very dry atmosphere, a person can build and hold a charge of several thousand volts when walking over rugs or working in certain manufacturing operations.

(1) <u>Formation of Charge</u>. Although a charge of this strength is unusual, the body does build up a charge during normal movement and work. Often the clothes and shoes of workers are moist enough to drain off the static electricity as fast as it is generated. The moisture provides a path for the charge to follow. Outer clothing, especially if they are made of wool or synthetic fiber, build a charge not only by absorbing part of the body charge but also by rubbing against the body and underwear. When the charged clothes are moved away from the body or taken off, the electrical tension or voltage increases to the dangerous point. If the clothes are wet with fuel, the danger is even more serious. Fuel-soaked clothes have been known to burst into flames as they were removed. Sparks can also be generated by worn footwear. Soles so worn that nails are exposed present a serious danger since fuel spills in refueling areas are common and fuel vapors near the ground ignite easily.

(2) <u>Safety Measures</u>. Before opening an aircraft fuel port or doing anything else that would let fuel vapors escape into the air, individuals must bond them-selves to the container by taking hold of it. If it is an aircraft or piece of metal equipment, a bare metal part can be held with both hands for a few seconds. Although this bonding will not completely discharge static electricity, it will equalize the charge on the body with the charge on the piece of equipment. No clothing is to be removed within 50 feet of a refueling operation or in an area where a flammable vapor-air mixture may exist. Individuals must not enter a flammable atmosphere after removing a garment, and least 10 minutes must pass before carrying the garment into such an atmosphere. If fuel gets on clothing, the person(s) must leave the refueling area as soon as refueling is completed and wet

the clothes with water before taking them off. If there is not enough water at the site to wet the clothes thoroughly, individuals can ground themselves to a piece of grounded equipment by taking hold of it before taking off the clothes. A skin irritation from fuel is not fatal; the fire that may follow a static discharge from clothing may be fatal.

H. Lightning. Lightning is a massive discharge of static electricity. Static charges build up in storm clouds until discharged as lightning.

(1) Dangers. The lightning stroke itself may present an ignition danger. In addition, lightning may suddenly release a charge trapped on an aircraft that is insulated from the ground. Such a freed charge may produce an arc of sufficient strength to ignite a flammable vapor-air mixture.

(2) Safety Measures. Stop refueling operations when there is lightning in the immediate area. Operations are not to be continued until the lightning has stopped.

FUEL SAMPLING AND TESTING - FUEL QUALITY CONTROL PROGRAM

C.1 General. Fuel Quality Control Program is referenced in the Handbook, chapter 3, Quality Control. This Appendix provides procedural guidance in the overall sampling and testing of fuels for effectively managing the Interior Fuel Quality Control Program.

C.2 Fuel Sampling and Testing Requirements. Sampling and testing of petroleum products must be accomplished during each phase of fuels transfer. This includes verification of fuel type and quality at the bulk dispensing facility pumping into fuel transport vehicles or trailers and at the fuel storage facility being operated by the bureau. It also includes any fuel source into the fuel vehicle or trailer which shall be conducting the into-aircraft refueling, and finally, fuel quality assurance prior to any into-aircraft fueling operations.

C.3 Testing. All petroleum testing shall be accomplished by trained personnel. These individuals may teach operators to perform API gravity, Aqua-Glo, and particulate contaminants by color indicator method or gravimetric tests on fuel owned or transferred by DOI bureaus. OAS personnel are available to make liaison visits and to give technical assistance to DOI bureaus they support. Additionally, bureaus shall designate and adequately train personnel to conduct these tests if qualified OAS personnel are unavailable.

C.4 Common Contamination Hazards. Quality control and surveillance testing and sampling are used to find common contamination hazards. The hazards which may affect aircraft are sediment, water, microbiological growth, and commingled fuel.

A. Sediment. Sediment from tanks, pipes, hoses, pumps, people, and the air contaminate fuel. The most common sediment found in aviation fuels are pieces of rust, paint, metal, rubber, dust, and sand. Sediment is classified by particle size.

(1) Coarse Sediment. Particles classified as course are 10 microns in size or larger (25,400 microns equal 1 inch). Coarse sediment settles out of fuel easily, and it can also be removed by adequate filtering. Particles of coarse sediment clog nozzle screens, other fine screens throughout the aircraft fuel system, and most dangerously, the fuel orifices of aircraft fuel injectors. Particles of this size also get wedged in sliding valve clearances and valve shoulders where they cause excessive wear in the field controls and fuel injection equipment.

(2) Fine Sediment. Particles classified as fine are smaller than 10 microns in size. Removing fine sediment by settling or filtering is effective only to a limited degree. The particles can be centrifuged out of fuel in a rotating chamber. Fine sediment accumulates in fuel controls and forms a dark, shellac-like surface on the sliding valves. It can also form a sludge-like material that causes fuel injection equipment to operate sluggishly. Particles of fine sediment are not visible to the naked eye, but they do scatter light. This light-scattering property makes them show up as point flashes of light or as a slight haze in the fuel.

B. Water. Either fresh or salt water may be in fuel. Water (fresh or salt) may be present as dissolved or free water.

(1) <u>Free Water</u>. Free Water can be removed from fuel by adequate filtering. It can be seen in the fuel as a cloud; emulsion; droplets; or in large amounts at the bottom of a tank, sample container, or filter/separator. Fresh or salty free water can freeze in the aircraft fuel system, can make certain aircraft instruments malfunction, and can corrode the components of the aircraft fuel system. (Salt water is more corrosive than fresh water.) Ice in an aircraft fuel system can make the engines fail.

(2) <u>Dissolved Water</u>. Dissolved water is water that has been absorbed by the fuel. It cannot be seen and cannot be separated out of the fuel by filtration or mechanical means. The danger of dissolved water is that it settles out as free water when the fuel is cooled to a temperature lower than that at which the water dissolved. Such a cooling of fuel is likely at high altitudes. Once freed, all the dangers of free water are present.

C. <u>Microbiological Growth</u>. If there is no water in the fuel, microbes cannot grow. Microbiological growth is brown, black, or gray and looks stringy or fibrous. It causes problems because these organisms hold rust and water in suspension and act as stabilizing agents for water-fuel emulsions. These suspensions cling to glass and metal and can cause false fuel quantity readings. They also make fuel controls operate sluggishly and make fuel flow dividers stick. Microbiological growth in aircraft fuel is a reliable indication that the fuel filters have failed, that the water has not been properly stripped from the fuel, or that the fuel storage tanks needs to be cleaned more frequently. Addition of FSII to JP-4 has helped curb microbiological growth. However, it is still necessary to remove all water from aviation fuel and aircraft fuel systems.

D. <u>Commingled Fuel</u>. Since each aircraft engine is designed to burn one particular type and grade of fuel, the consequences of using a mixture of different fuels can range from small variations in engine performance to total loss of power and engine failure. The consequences of commingling depend on the physical properties of the fuel.

C.5 <u>Filters/Separators and Single Element Monitors with Absorbent Media</u>. Filter/separators help to keep fuel clean and free from water. When fuel is left in the dispensing hose at the end of the day's operation, it should be recirculated through the filter/separator before operations resume. Refer to Chapter 4, <u>Filtration</u>, for additional information, specifications, and standards.

C.6 <u>Sampling and Testing Frequency</u>.

A. <u>Fuel in a System or Refueler</u>. The fuel in tank or refueler must be sampled and tested before use and again when the filter elements of the filter/separator on the system or refueler are changed. Refuelers should be tested during the daily pre-operational recirculation of fuel. This sampling and testing should be performed before any fuel is dispensed.

B. <u>Fuel in Aircraft Tank(s)</u>. A visual check of the fuel in aircraft tanks shall be made by the flight crew before each flight. The sample should be taken after the fuel tank sumps have been drained. The sample should be drawn in a clean, clear glass container. The size of the sample may vary depending on the condition of the fuel. If contamination shows in the sample, more fuel should be drawn. If water, sediment, or any other suspicious matter is visible in the fuel after 1 quart or more is drawn the aircraft shall not be flown and the Chief Pilot or Supervisor shall be consulted.

C.7 <u>Laboratory Testing</u>. Laboratory testing ensures that the fuel's quality meets specifications; that unknown products are identified; that existing or potential contamination causes are identified; that unfavorable field test results are corroborated; and that off-specification fuels are not used. Each using bureau should submit petroleum samples to OAS for coordination with the laboratory for testing by qualified technicians. These samples are submitted as follows:

➢When fuel quality is questionable.

➢After any aircraft accident or serious incident in which the engine failed or engine failure is suspected.

C.8 <u>System Sampling and Testing</u>. Certain minimum requirements for testing at the user level must be carried out before refueling aircraft and before flight. The scope of the testing is restricted by the availability of testing equipment suitable for use in field situations, availability of trained personnel to conduct the test, and by the short time frame in which test results must be obtained. This testing identifies the most common forms of aircraft fuel contamination. These are commingling, particulate matter, and water.

   A. <u>Testing From The Fuel Source</u>. Fuel supplies must be tested to confirm their identities (API gravity test); to detect water (Aqua-Glo test); and to detect particulate contaminates by color comparative ratings. The aviation fuel contamination test kit is designed to provide a final check on aviation fuel just before fueling of an aircraft. It includes the API gravity test, the Aqua-Glo test, and the Millipore test (a test for particulate contaminates). The kit is usually operated by trained individuals.

      (1)   <u>Fuel Classification (API Gravity Test)</u>. Each type and grade of fuel has a particular API gravity range. The API gravity test indicates whether a fuel is actually what it is supposed to be. It is used hand in hand with visual examination. A visual check differentiates fuels by color: JP-4, JP-5, and JP-8, Jet A, etc., are clear to amber; and AVGAS, grade 100/130, is green, and 100 low-lead (100LC) is blue. The API gravity test confirms the color identification. This test is necessary because the dyes used in fuels may lose color with age or when subjected to heat. The API gravity test is a measure of the average specific gravity or weight of the hydrocarbons (molecules) present.

      (2)   <u>Water Detection (Aqua-Glo Test)</u>. The presence of water in a fuel is tested with the automotive/aviation fuel water detector kit, commonly called the Aqua-Glo kit. Aviation fuels may not be used if they contain more than 15 parts per million (PPM) of water. The Aqua-Glo water detection test checks to see that the filter/separator is working properly. If a reading is below the maximum allowable amount (15 PPM), the fuel is within limits. If the test shows more than 15 PPM of water in the sample, the fuel is "off specification." This indicates the filter failed or that there is a malfunction in the system. The fuel, and the system or refueler pumping it, should be removed from service immediately for further examination. The fuel must be segregated and sampled.

The sample may be sent to OAS to coordinate laboratory tests called for by its specification. The equipment must be inspected to see if any source of water is present. The filter must be opened and its filter elements removed and replaced. Before the system or refueler may be placed back in service, it must be retested to be sure that the water content of the fuel is below the maximum reading.

(3)   Fibrous Material. Samples of fuel that are to be dispensed to aircraft should contain no more than 10 fibers when a 1-quart sample is visually examined. When more than 10 fibers can be seen, the filter or filter/separator elements are not functioning properly. Corrective action should be taken.

(4)   Filter Membrane Color Ratings. Filter membrane color ratings are used to determine the quality of aviation turbine fuels (its particulate contamination). Appendix C discusses the use and procedures of this test.

(5) Gravimetric (Membrane Filtration). Using a field sampling kit, a measured volume of fuel is passed through a pair of filter membranes in a field monitor. The field monitor is then removed from the field sampling kit and forwarded to a qualified laboratory for weighing.

B. Testing Fuel in Aircraft Tanks. Fuel in aircraft tanks must be checked by the aircraft crew before flight operations begin. Taking a preflight sample is the only way of ensuring that the fuel on board does not contain water or other visible contaminants. (The sample must be taken after the fuel tank sumps have been drained. Check for contamination by taking a sample from fuel sumps and filters in accordance with the operator's manual.) Although visual checks safeguard against and warn of contamination, they do not ensure that the checked product meets all requirements of its specification. When a visual check indicates that the fuel may be contaminated, the aircraft should not be permitted to fly and the fuel sample should be sent to the supporting laboratory for testing. Any remaining fuel in storage should be isolated and not used until test reports are received. Any fuel that fails a visual check should be segregated and held until laboratory test results are received. To visually
check a fuel, draw a sample in a clean sample bottle and look for the items described below.

(1)   Color. The color of an aviation fuel depends on its type and grade. Leaded fuels must be dyed, so AVGAS is dyed differently for different grades. Grade 100/130 is dyed green and grade 100 low-lead is dyed blue. Jet fuels, because they are unleaded, are not dyed They may be any color from water white to amber. Proper color indicates freshness and uniformity, but not necessarily quality. An off color or color of the wrong intensity does not always mean that the fuel is "off specification," but it does mean that contamination signs should be looked for.

(2)   Cleanliness and Brightness. The fuel should be clean and bright. Cleanliness and brightness are distinct from fuel color. Clean means without visible sediment, cloud, haze, emulsion, or free water. Bright means having the characteristic sparkled of clean, dry fuel in transmitted light.

(3)   Cloud or Haze. Ordinarily, a cloud or haze in fuel indicates the presence of water, but cloudiness can be caused by large amounts of fine sediment. Cloudy fuel is not acceptable for use in aircraft. When a clean, bright fuel cools, a light cloud may form. Such a cloud indicates that dissolved water has separated out into a very small amount of free water. Since free water is not acceptable in aviation fuels, the fuel should be rejected. If a cloud is present in a fuel after it has been passed through a filter/separator system, the filter elements in the filter/separator should be replaced. Also, the source tank should be stripped of both water and emulsion. Cloudy fuel should be recirculated through fresh filter elements. A precipitation cloud can be removed by a filter/separator that is working properly.

(4) Sediment. To be visible to the naked eye as specks, sediment particles must be larger than 40 microns. Visible sediment particles in a sample indicate that the filter/separator is not working properly; that there is a source of contamination downstream of the filter/separator; or that the sample container was not cleaned properly. In a sample of clean fuel, no sediments should be visible. However, even with the most efficient filter/separator and careful fuel handling, occasionally there will be visible sediment particles in fuel. This sediment will normally be in the form of an extremely fine powder, rouge, or silt.

(5) Water. Entrained water may appear as a cloud or haze and it may settle out. Free water may be visible as droplets or at the bottom of the sample container. If any free or entrained water is present, the fuel is unacceptable.

(6) Fibrous Material. A quart sample of acceptable aviation fuel should not contain more than 10 fibers. The presence of more than 10 fibers-per-quart indicates that the filter/separator from the servicing vehicle is not working properly or that the filter elements are breaking down. The fibers can be detected visually, but a specific count can be determined only by laboratory testing.